OTHER BOOKS BY ALEX MITCHELL

Quizzin' Nine-Nine: A Brooklyn Nine-Nine Quiz Book

Parks & Interrogation: A Parks & Recreation Quiz Book

Q & AC-12: A Line of Duty Quiz Book

Know Your Schitt: A Schitt's Creek Quiz Book

Examilton: A Hamilton Musical Quiz Book

The BTS Quiz Book

The Ariana Grande Quiz Book

360 Questions to Test a True Ariana Grande Fan

Published by Beartown Press

Copyright © 2020 Alex Mitchell

This book is unofficial, unauthorised and in no way associated with Ariana Grande or any of her artistic or commercial endeavours. It is purely a fun trivia book designed to test the knowledge of Arianators.

ISBN 9798675667048

For you, you lovely reader.

"You should never stop believing in something, and you shouldn't listen to anyone who tells you otherwise."

Contents

Personal Facts 1	10
Personal Facts 2	11
Personal Facts 3	12
Personal Facts 4	13
Collaborations/Duets 1	15
Collaborations/Duets 2	17
Acting	19
Movie/TV Show Soundtracks	21
Merchandise	23
Famous Friends 1	25
Famous Friends 2	27
Songs 1	29
Songs 2	30
Songs 3	32
Albums 1	34
Albums 2	36
Music Videos 1	38

Music Videos 2	40
Lyrics 1	42
Lyrics 2	44
Lyrics 3	46
Lyrics 4	48
Feuds	50
Awards 1	52
Awards 2	53
Chart Success	55
Guest Appearances 1	57
Guest Appearances 2	59
Guest Appearances 3	61
Quotes 1	63
Quotes 2	65
Cat Valentine	67
Diva Behavior	68
Miscellaneous 1	70
Miscellaneous 2	72
Anagrams	73

ANSWERS 75

Introduction

Millions of fans. Hundreds of songs. One incredible superstar.

And 360 questions about her journey since she came *Bang Bang* into our lives. This is the ultimate Ariana Grande quiz book.

Let's get started – and don't worry if you don't get every single question right. After all, in the words of Ariana: "Imperfection is beauty, madness is genius, and it's better to be absolutely ridiculous than absolutely boring."

Enjoy the quiz.

Alex Mitchell

Personal Facts 1

1. In which year was Ariana Grande born?

2. In which state was Ariana born?

3. On which popular social media platform was Ariana first discovered?

4. What is Ariana's brother's name?

5. Which fruit is Ariana allergic to?

6. Where did Ariana celebrate her 21st birthday?

7. Which cartoon character was the inspiration behind Ariana's name?

8. Which common household pet is Ariana allergic to?

9. In 2015 what type of treat did Ariana get in trouble for licking at a bakery?

10. Ariana made her debut TV performance singing the national anthem for which NHL team's home game in 2002?

Answers on page 77

Personal Facts 2

1. What is Ariana Grande's mother's name?

2. What is Ariana Grande's zodiac sign?

3. What date is Ariana's birthday?

4. What is Ariana's natural hair color?

5. What is Ariana's favorite color?

6. What is Ariana's favorite animal?

7. After the success of 7 Rings, Ariana wanted a tattoo of the song title in Japanese on her palm. Unfortunately there was some miscommunication - what does the tattoo translate as?

8. What did Ariana take care of for her ex-boyfriend Mac Miller after he died in 2018?

9. What is Ariana's favorite holiday?

10. Why did the ponytail become Ariana's signature look for many years?

Answers on page 78

Personal Facts 3

1. What is the name of Ariana's 2018 4-part documentary?

2. Which approach to food and eating does Ariana practice?

3. What is Ariana's father's name?

4. As of 2020, how many Teen Choice Awards has Ariana received?

5. Who has Ariana named as the key influence on her career?

6. On which season of Big Brother was Ariana's brother Frankie a contestant?

7. Which Harry Potter character did Ariana name her dog after?

8. Where on her body is Ariana's birthmark located?

9. What was Ariana's favorite subject in school?

10. Ariana once said she had her first celebrity crush at the age of 3 - who was it?

Answers on page 79

Personal Facts 4

1. Which bird did Ariana say was the cutest? Penguin

2. Which health concern does Ariana need to be cautious about? She is hypoglycemic

3. Where did Ariana put her hands in cement in 2015? Planet Hollywood, New York

4. Ariana's Put Your Hearts Up music video was released on what special calendar date? Valentine's Day, 14th February

5. Which Sam & Cat co-star accidentally made Ariana's phone number public? Jennette McCurdy

6. What did Ariana say her mother used to think her daughter would become when she grew up? A serial killer! We think she's joking

7. On December 10, 2011 what social media milestone did Ariana achieve? 1 million Twitter followers

8. Who were Ariana's two fashion inspirations while growing up? Marilyn Monroe and Audrey Hepburn

9. What 3 items did Ariana collect as a kid? Stuffed animals, hockey pucks and Halloween masks

10. Who is Ariana's manager? Scooter Braun

Answers on page 80

Collaborations/Duets 1

1. In 2020 Ariana was featured on which singer's hit track Rain on Me?
2. What song did Ariana collaborate with Childish Gambino on for her album My Everything?
3. What song did Ariana team up with Justin Bieber for during the 2020 pandemic?
4. What was the first song that Ariana collaborated with Nicki Minaj on?
5. Who joined Ariana for Popular Song?
6. John Legend and Ariana teamed up for a song named after which Disney movie?
7. Which female rapper joined Ariana for the song Problem?
8. Ariana teamed up with Socialhouse following the success of her album Thank You Next in 2019 for which hit song?
9. In 2019 Ariana joined Lizzo for a remix of which hit song?

10. In 2018 Ariana collaborated with Nicki Minaj on a song named after which piece of furniture?

Answers on page 81

Collaborations/Duets 2

1. Which friend joined Ariana for the song Monopoly?
2. In 2016 Ariana collaborated with Stevie Wonder for which song?
3. Who joined Ariana for a duet on Leave Me Lonely?
4. Which track from the My Everything album did Ariana collaborate with The Weeknd on?
5. What was the name of the duet with Mac Miller that Ariana considers her first single?
6. Which popular singer joined Ariana Grande and Nicki Minaj on the track Bang Bang?
7. Who does Ariana team up with for the holiday track A Hand For Mrs Claus?
8. Which female rapper had a short bit on the Sweetener track Borderline?
9. Which Norwegian producer did Ariana collaborate with for Quit?

10. Who joined Ariana for the song Hands on Me?

Answers on page 82

Acting

1. What was the first Broadway production that Ariana was cast in, at the age of 15?

2. Which character did Ariana play in Sam & Cat?

3. Ariana's character in Sam &Cat was originally from which Nickelodeon TV show?

4. In the TV series Scream Queens, each sorority sister is given a Chanel number as a name - which does Ariana's character go by?

5. Which character did Ariana provide the voice of in the animated Nickelodeon TV series Winx Club?

6. Ariana played a cheerleader named Amanda in which TV movie?

7. In 2016 Ariana started in Hairspray Live as which character?

8. How many seasons of Scream Queens did Ariana feature in?

9. In which movie did Ariana cameo as a participant in an X-rated adult group?

10. Ariana appears in an uncredited role as an alien in which movie?

Answers on page 83

Movie/TV Show Soundtracks

1. Which Ariana Grande song was performed on the TV series Glee?

2. Which movie was the song Don't Call Me Angel recorded for?

3. Which 2 singers did Ariana collaborate with on Don't Call Me Angel?

4. Which Ariana Grande song was featured on Pitch Perfect 2?

5. What song did Ariana perform for the animated film Sing?

6. Which Ariana Grande song is featured on Just Dance 2020?

7. What song did Ariana perform for the animated film Trolls?

8. Which 2016 movie used a remix of the song All My Love?

9. What Ariana Grande song was playing on the TV show Pretty Little Liars while Ashley Benson's character is auditioning for a dance competition?

10. Which song did Ariana write for the 2020 movie Work It?

Answers on page 84

Merchandise

1. What was the name of the drink that Starbucks collaborated with Ariana Grande on in 2019?

2. What was the name of Ariana's first perfume?

3. When did Ariana release her first perfume?

4. What was the first perfume that Ariana named after one of her albums?

5. There is something in the sky that Ariana is so fascinated with that she named a perfume after it. What is the name of the perfume?

6. Which Ariana Grande perfume, released in 2019, came in a broken-heart case?

7. Which Ariana Grande perfume released in 2016 came with a pink pom-pom on the side of the bottle?

8. From 2015 to 2017, to the nearest million dollars, how much money did Ariana's fragrance company make?

9. Which is the real name of an Ariana Grande fragrance: Sunlight, Midnight, Moonlight or Oyster Light?

10. In 2019, what was Ariana's top selling perfume?

Answers on page 85

Famous Friends 1

1. What castmate from Ariana's first Broadway production did she later work with on the set of Victorious?

2. Who was the first singer Ariana saw in concert?

3. Which comedian did Ariana have a whirlwind engagement to in 2018?

4. Which 2020 Grammy Award winner thought Ariana should have taken her place for Album of the Year?

5. Which singer did Ariana Grande join for a performance in their pajamas in 2015?

6. Who was the first ex-lover that Ariana mentions in the song Thank U, Next?

7. Which friend joined Ariana and her mom for a reenactment of a scene from The Waterboy during the 2020 pandemic?

8. Which male popstar friend did Ariana spontaneously invite onstage with her during one of her 2019 Coachella performances?

9. Which actress gained support of Ariana in 2020 after receiving bullying messages online from fans about her relationship?

10. Which famous Canadian has Ariana named as her favorite comedic actor?

Answers on page 86

Famous Friends 2

1. Which famous friend once said that Ariana owned pop music?

2. Which past co-star showed some jealousy on air when other castmates were talking about how Ariana sings everything?

3. Which singing friend helped Ariana to write Thank U, Next?

4. As of 2020, what has been the bestselling Ariana Grande and Nicki Minaj collaboration?

5. Which single-word statement did Ariana deliver in a since-deleted tweet after Cardi B brought home the 2019 Grammy for Best Rap Album?

6. From 2013 to 2020, which artist has Ariana performed with the most times live?

7. If Ariana won the lottery, which friend did she say she would like to buy a house to live in with?

8. Which friend did Ariana get her driver's license permit with?

9. What is the name of the YouTube channel that Ariana once made with Matt Bennett and Elizabeth Gillies?

10. Which ex-boyfriend said he had the worst line on Ariana's track Thank U, Next?

Answers on page 87

Songs 1

1. Which hit Ariana song was released in November 2018?

2. What was the first hit single off of the Sweetener album?

3. Which Ariana song was released in July 2019?

4. Which one of Ariana's then-boyfriends got a song named after him on the Sweetener album in 2018?

5. What was the lead single off of the 2014 album My Everything?

6. What was the name of Ariana's 2013 holiday hit?

7. What is the name of Ariana's 2011 hit single?

8. What was the song Ariana recorded with Mac Miller in 2016?

9. Childish Gambino featured Ariana on which 2020 song?

10. Which single did Ariana record with Nicki Minaj in 2018?

Answers on page 88

Songs 2

1. Who was featured at the beginning of Ariana's song NASA?

2. Which song on the Thank U, Next album does Ariana's grandmother make an appearance on?

3. Which song represented Ariana's healing after the 2017 Manchester attack?

4. Ariana doesn't like the negativity brought on by diss tracks. What is the name of the anti-diss track that Ariana released in 2018?

5. Which song on the Yours Truly album has the longest runtime?

6. Which song on the Yours Truly album has the shortest runtime?

7. Which song on the Thank U, Next album has the longest runtime?

8. Which song on the Thank U, Next album has the shortest runtime?

9. Which song on the My Everything album has the longest runtime?

10. Which track on the My Everything album has the shortest runtime?

Answers on page 89

Songs 3

1. Which song on the Sweetener album has the longest runtime?

2. Which song on the Sweetener album has the shortest runtime?

3. Which song on the Dangerous Woman album has the longest runtime?

4. Which song on the Dangerous Woman album has the shortest runtime?

5. Which song starts off with Ariana singing "Don't need permission, made my decision to test my limits"?

6. Which famous song does 7 Rings sample?

7. How many songs are on Ariana's live album K Bye For Now?

8. What is the name of the first track on Ariana's debut album?

9. What was the final track on the Thank U, Next album?

10. What is track five on the Sweetener album?

Answers on page 90

Albums 1

1. What is the name of Ariana's 2015 Christmas-themed album? Christmas & Chill

2. Who was the producer behind the album Yours Truly? Babyface

3. How many copies did My Everything sell in its first week? 169,000

4. What is the name of Ariana's debut studio album? Yours Truly

5. What is the name of Ariana's third studio album? Dangerous Woman

6. What label were Ariana's first five studio albums recorded under? Republic

7. What is the name of Ariana's 2019 live album? K Bye For Now

8. What was the original name for Ariana's debut album? Daydreamin'

9. How long did Ariana spend writing the songs for the Thank U, Next album? 2 weeks

10. How long did Ariana spend on her first studio album? 3 years

Answers on page 91

Albums 2

1. Which of her albums was Ariana describing when she said that it is about "bringing light to a situation or to someone's life"? Sweetener

2. Which was the first studio album that Ariana took the lead in writing her own songs? Sweetener

3. On which album cover does it look like Ariana Grande is defying gravity on her stool? My Everything

4. On which album cover does Ariana trade her signature high ponytail for a bleach blonde low ponytail? Sweetener

5. On which album cover is Ariana wearing a latex mask with bunny ears? Dangerous Woman

6. What was the first album cover of Ariana's that wasn't in black and white? Sweetener

7. Prior to 2020, Ariana had two number 1 albums within 6 months of each other - what were they? Sweetener and Thank U, Next

8. How many duets/collabs were on the Sweetener album? 3

9. How many tracks are on the Thank U, Next album? 12

10. Which album does the song Break Free feature on? My Everything

Answers on page 92

Music Videos 1

1. Which Riverdale castmate made an appearance in the Breakup With Your Girlfriend, I'm Bored music video?

2. Which famous Kardashian made an appearance in the Thank U Next music video?

3. Which 2020 Ariana music video had a star-studded cast including Demi Lovato and Mila Kunis?

4. Which Mean Girls star reprised their role for the Thank U Next music video?

5. Who directed the Problem music video?

6. Who directed the Rain on Me music video?

7. How many music videos did Ariana come out with in 2013?

8. What song did Ariana and Nicki Minaj do a music video for in 2016?

9. What 2019 Lil Dicky music video did Ariana make an appearance in?

10. From 2013-2020 which singer has Ariana Grande made the most music videos with?

Answers on page 93

Music Videos 2

1. Which music video pays homage to Ariana's favorite chick flicks?

2. Which of Ariana Grande's dogs made a cameo in her 7 Rings music video?

3. Which 2015 music video does Ariana have a head of bright white hair?

4. Which Legally Blonde star made a cameo in one of Ariana's videos?

5. In which of Ariana's 2020 music videos did Gwyneth Paltrow make an appearance?

6. Which music video sees Ariana switch looks with the artist she collaborated with?

7. In which 2013 music video does Ariana wear fun animal hats?

8. What was Ariana Grande's first music video?

9. Which Victorious co-star was brushing their teeth in the Thank U, Next video?

10. What was the first music video in which Ariana wore bangs?

Answers on page 94

Lyrics 1

Can you identify the song from the lyric?

1. "Head in the clouds. Got no weight on my shoulders"?
2. "And boy I got ya. 'Cause tonight I'm making deals with the devil. And I know it's gonna get me in trouble. Just as long as you know you got me"?
3. "Comin' out, even when it's rainin' down. Can't stop now, can't stop so shut your mouth"?
4. "If you confess, you might get blessed. See if you deserve what comes next. I'm tellin' you the way I like it, how I want it"?
5. "One taught me love. One taught me patience. And one taught me pain. Now, I'm so amazing"?
6. "My smile is beamin', my skin is gleamin'. The way it shine, I know you've seen it"?

7. "Stayin' up all night, order me pad Thai. Then we gon' sleep 'til noon. Me with no makeup, you in the bathtub. Bubbles and bubbly, ooh"?

8. "What goes around comes around. And if it goes up, it comes down. I know you mad 'cause I found out. Want you to feel what I feel right now"?

9. "I only want to die alive. Never by the hands of a broken heart"?

10. "You give me that special kind of something. Want it all the time, need it every day"?

Answers on page 95

Lyrics 2

Can you identify the song from the lyric?

1. "The ones that love me, I tend to leave behind. If you know about me and choose to stay, then take this pleasure and take away this pain"?
2. ""Strawberry lingerie, waiting for you"?
3. "I can tell you're curious, it's written on your lips"?
4. "Why can't we just play for keeps? Practically on my knees"?
5. "I'm obsessive and I love too hard. Good at overthinking with my heart"?
6. "The words don't ever come out right. I get all tongue-tied, I can't explain what I'm feeling"?
7. "Standing in the field with your pretty pompoms, now you're working at the movies selling popular corn"?

8. "She might have let you hold her hand in school, but I'm'a show you how to graduate"?

9. "Certain as the sun. Rising in the east. Tale as old as time"?

10. "Oh baby look what you started. The temperature is rising in here"?

Answers on page 96

Lyrics 3

Can you identify the song from the lyric?

1. "I'm locked and loaded. Completely focused, my mind is open"?
2. "Last night I met you boy when I was asleep. You're such a dream to me"?
3. "Love me, thank you, leave me. Put it down, it's time to go"?
4. "Just one match in the lights of the city"?
5. "My energy and my attitude don't really coincide. I'm staying mad all day so we can let it out tonight"?
6. "Boy you making me feel so lucky, finally the stars are aligned"?
7. "When life deals us cards, make everything taste like salt"?

8. "Teardrops on my face, water like misery, let it wash away my sins"?

9. "Cause I can't give it away if he won't be here next year"?

10. "I know that it breaks your heart when I cry again, over him"?

Answers on page 97

Lyrics 4

Can you identify the song from the lyric?

1. "We don't need to go nowhere tonight, it's you and I, we'll be alright"?
2. "I've been doing stupid things, wilder than I ever have been"?
3. "I've been worried about you baby, running outta time, wishin' you would come save me"?
4. "Tonight I'm going to lose, don't play me, just kiss me"?
5. "I don't want to be too much, but I don't want to miss your touch"?
6. "How could I just forget, made everything from nothing because time was all we spent"?
7. "You walked in and caught my attention, never seen a man with so much dimension"?

8. "My imagination's too creative, they see demon, I see angel"?

9. "I read the things they write about me, hear what they're saying on tv, it's crazy"?

10. "My life is so controlled by the what ifs, girl what's wrong with you? Come back down"?

Answers on page 98

Feuds

1. Which rapper accused Ariana of buying her Billboard status in 2020?

2. Which Victorious co-star did Ariana have tension with?

3. Which outspoken rapper had some words for Ariana in 2018 after she suggested he cool an argument with Drake to "let the ladies shine"?

4. Which songstress earned a spot in Ariana's bad books after accusing her of using her sexuality to sell songs?

5. Which actor had an army of Ariana Grande fans flood his Twitter comments after he decided to use the platform to insult the popstar in 2018?

6. Which model took a jab at Ariana's cat-ear headband on Twitter, saying "I love your cat ear headband it alerts me to immediately hate you"?

7. Which rapper claimed Ariana stole her track 7 Rings from them and called her a thief on Twitter?

8. Which ex blocked Ariana on social media after their breakup?

9. Which UK group did Piers Morgan insult to enrage Ariana?

10. Which beauty vlogger claimed Ariana was "the rudest celebrity" in 2018, even though they had never actually met?

Answers on page 99

Awards 1

1. In 2015, how many MTV Millennial Awards did Ariana win?

2. Which album won a 2019 Grammy for Best Pop Vocal?

3. Which song won a 2014 MTV Europe Music Award for best song?

4. What Billboard award did Ariana win in 2019?

5. Which social media award did Ariana win in 2015?

6. What Billboard Music Award did Ariana win in 2014?

7. Which Ariana song won a Teen Choice Award for 2019 Choice Pop Song?

8. Which tour won 2017's Teen Choice Tour Award?

9. In 2015 and 2017 Ariana took home a Radio Disney Music Award in which category?

10. In 2014 she won which People's Choice award?

Answers on page 100

Awards 2

1. Which American Music Award did Ariana bring home in 2016?

2. Which 2018 iHeartRadio Music Award did Ariana bring home?

3. Which award did Sweetener win at the 2019 iHeartRadio Music Awards?

4. Which Shorty award did Ariana receive in 2019?

5. Which social-media-focused Teen Choice award did Ariana win in both 2017 and 2018?

6. From 2014-2016, Ariana earned the win for which Teen Choice Award category?

7. For which song did Ariana win Favorite Song at the Kids Choice Award in 2019?

8. Which Ariana music video won the 2019 MTV Video Music Award for Best Art Direction?

9. Which Ariana music video won the 2018 MTV Video Music award for best Pop Video?

10. In 2013, which American Music Award did Ariana win?

Answers on page 101

Chart Success

1. How long did it take for Ariana's first studio album to reach #1 in the iTunes Store Charts in over 30 countries (US included)?

2. Which 2015 Ariana Grande hit debuted at number 7 on the Billboard Hot 100?

3. Which position did Ariana's album Dangerous Woman debut at on the Billboard 200?

4. Why did Ariana make Billboard charts history in 2016?

5. During the summer of 2014, how many singles did Ariana have on the charts at one time?

6. In which chart position did the 2019 hit song 7 Rings debut in the US?

7. Which album did Ariana break Billboard records with, by having songs holding the 1, 2, and 3 chart spots for the first time once The Beatles in 1964?

8. Ariana had a record-breaking year in 2019 - but by the end of that year, which of her songs had become the biggest success of all-time on the charts?

9. In 2019, for how many weeks did the song 7 Rings stay at number 1 on the Billboard charts?

10. Where on the Billboard charts did the 2019 song Break Up With Your Girlfriend, I'm Bored peak at?

Answers on page 102

Guest Appearances 1

1. On which season of Ru Paul's Drag Race was Ariana a guest judge on?

2. Which animated series did Ariana lend her voice to for an episode in 2014?

3. On a 2016 appearance on Jimmy Fallon show, what animal did Ariana say she would want to be?

4. In 2015 what character did Ariana play in a guest appearance on Jimmy Fallon's "Ew"?

5. Which animal was printed on Ariana's dress during that 2015 "Ew" appearance?

6. Whose concert did Ariana make a surprise appearance at in January 2016?

7. Who did Ariana join for a round of Carpool Karaoke in 2018?

8. On a 2016 SNL performance, Ariana was able to point to her house out the window. Where does she claim to live?

9. In 2020 she made an appearance on which Jim Carrey show?

10. What type of fairy did Ariana play in that appearance?

Answers on page 103

Guest Appearances 2

1. On which television network did Ariana start her acting career?

2. What is the name of the 2018 program in Ariana which appeared, where she had to name song lyrics?

3. What was the name of the benefit concert Ariana hosted after the 2017 Manchester attack?

4. What 2015 Disney TV event did she participate in?

5. What 2015 female lead movie did Ariana have an uncredited appearance in?

6. Which 2015 festival did Ariana make an appearance at?

7. How many times did Ariana appear on Live with Kelly and Ryan between 2013 and 2015?

8. Between 2014 and 2016, how many times was Ariana a guest on Saturday Night Live?

9. Which 2020 documentary series did Ariana feature in an episode of?

10. How many episodes of The Tonight Show With Jimmy Fallon did Ariana appear in between 2015 and 2020?

Answers on page 104

Guest Appearances 3

1. In 2016, which fashion event did Ariana attend as a musical guest?

2. Which year saw a Victoria Secret model almost knock Ariana over with her wings while on stage?

3. What word did Ariana later use to describe getting hit in the face with a Victoria Secret Angel's wings?

4. Who was the Victoria Secret model that accidentally hit Ariana with her wings?

5. In a 2018 episode of SNL, who did Ariana imitate for a game of Celebrity Family Feud?

6. What was the name of the song Ariana performed on a 2016 episode of SNL to poke fun at celebrity culture?

7. What was the name of the exclusive female empowerment song Ariana performed on a 2016 episode of SNL?

8. In a 2016 SNL skit called Tidal, Ariana plays a character who fills the gaps when a music streaming service goes down. Who is the one artist her character refuses to sing the songs of?

9. Which female superhero did Ariana play in a 2014 episode of SNL?

10. Which 2018 SNL Cut For Time skit did Ariana appear in?

Answers on page 105

Quotes 1

1. Which song was Ariana talking about when she said: "I'm tired of living in a world where women are mostly referred to as a man's past, present or future property/possession"?
2. Which album was Ariana talking about when she describes it as being about: "Someone who is not afraid to take a risk and be themselves"?
3. Which song was Ariana talking about when she said: "The concept that we wanted to explore was the disorientation that you go through in life"?
4. Ariana Grande say that she doesn't regret any of her life decisions, because with every choice, she has learned what?
5. What does Ariana describe as being one of the most beautiful, but also scary things in life?
6. Fill in the blank in this popular Ariana Grande quote: "Love your _____"?

7. Fill in the blank in this popular Ariana Grande quote: "It's better to be absolutely ridiculous than absolutely _"?

8. Fill in the blank in this popular Ariana Grande quote: "When someone is hurting, be there. We could all use a little ____"?

9. Fill in the blank in this popular Ariana Grande quote: "Own your ____"?

10. What is one thing Ariana notices that people will find any reason to feel and wishes they would stop spreading so much of it?

Answers on page 106

Quotes 2

1. What does Ariana claim trained her to be prepared for anything?

2. What does Ariana Grande say everyone should do regarding their mistakes?

3. Fill in the blank in this popular Ariana Grande quote: "Girls, ____ yourselves"?

4. What does Ariana suggest you do when you are faced with something ugly?

5. Fill in the blank in this popular Ariana Grande quote: "Plant love, grow ____"?

6. Fill in the blank in this popular Ariana Grande quote: "Imperfection is beauty. Madness is ____"?

7. Fill in the blank in this popular Ariana Grande quote: "Don't take everything so ____ and just be happier"?

8. Ariana believes you should only be with someone if they make you feel like what?

9. Fill in the blank in this popular Ariana Grande quote: "You don't have to have much to show you ____"?

10. What is Ariana Grande's only fashion rule?

Answers on page 107

Cat Valentine

1. How many different shows did Ariana Grande play the character of Cat Valentine in?
2. Who did Cat live with when her parents left for Idaho?
3. What color is Cat Valentine's giraffe?
4. When Cat had no family left to live with, who became her roommate?
5. Who is Cat Valentine's best friend?
6. Who is Cat Valentine's longtime crush?
7. Who was the inspiration behind the character of Cat Valentine?
8. What is one simple thing Cat often forgets to do?
9. What food did Cat Valentine need a book on so she could learn to make it?
10. How many times was Cat Valentine arrested?

Answers on page 108

Diva Behaviour

1. What side of her face does Ariana want all her interviews done on?

2. Which Scream Queens co-star did Ariana unfollow on social media after it was revealed that this star was a bully to cast members on the set of other shows/movies?

3. Which pop star did Ariana throw shade at for lip-syncing their 2015 Jingle Ball performance?

4. Who claimed to walk in and find Ariana Grande with their fiancé in their 2016 tell-all book?

5. What mistake did Ariana make for her 2015 scheduled performance on the Jonathon Ross Show?

6. In 2014, which interviewer said that Ariana Grande was her least favorite person to work with?

7. Which member of the band The Cab publicly tweeted about Ariana's "disrespectful" behavior at their show together?

8. Which friend turned enemy claimed working with Ariana sucked the life out of her?

9. In 2014 Ariana left a fan disappointed when she apparently stayed for only 15 seconds of their meet and greet. Allegedly Ariana was not a fan of what the girl presented to win the contest. What did this girl enter in the contest?

10. In 2014 New York Daily News reported that Ariana was accused of saying something nasty about her fans in an elevator - what was it?

Answers on page 109

Miscellaneous 1

1. Which Scream Queens co-star said that she went to the same school as Ariana?

2. What animal was Ariana's character in Scream Queens upset about not seeing in hell?

3. In 2018 which pop star gave a shout out to Ariana after she realized just how heavy high ponytail extensions can be?

4. Which popstar accidentally scratched Ariana Grande when they were working together in 2020?

5. In 2014 which pop star couldn't control her laughter over something Ariana's friend said during Ariana's iHeartRadio performance?

6. Who plays the sorority sister in Scream Queens that Ariana's character pushes down the stairs?

7. Which former Pretty Little Liars actress showed a tremendous amount of support for Ariana on her social media accounts after the 2019 release of her Thank U, Next album and Starbucks drink release?

8. Which politician has Ariana been open about endorsing in 2020?

9. Who joined Ariana on stage at the One Love Manchester benefit for a cover of Don't Dream It's Over?

10. What song did Ariana sing with Coldplay for the One Love Manchester benefit?

Answers on page 110

Miscellaneous 2

1. How many people attended the One Love Manchester benefit Ariana organized in 2017?

2. For which cause was One Love Manchester held?

3. What was the last song Ariana sang on the set of the One Love Manchester benefit?

4. How many tracks are on the Yours Truly album?

5. How many songs did Ariana do at One Love Manchester?

6. Is Ariana's hair naturally straight, wavy, or curly?

7. How old was Ariana when she made her TV debut?

8. What year did Victorious first air?

9. In which year did Ariana join YouTube?

10. Which singing idol of Ariana's was able to make an appearance at her One Love Manchester benefit in 2017, singing Hide and Seek?

Answers on page 111

Anagrams

Can you scramble these Ariana song titles?

1. Forecast Rottenly?

2. Marveled Hero?

3. Mania Dogs Ow?

4. Babysat Heated Tune?

5. Hosting?

6. A Free Kerb?

7. No Hotdogging?

8. Extant Hunk?

9. Dab Aide?

10. Iron Mane?

Answers on page 112

ANSWERS

Answer Sheet: Personal Facts 1

1. 1993

2. Florida

3. YouTube

4. Frankie

5. Bananas

6. Walt Disney World

7. Princess Oriana from Felix the Cat

8. Cats

9. A doughnut - who can blame the girl!

10. Florida Panthers

Answer Sheet: Personal Facts 2

1. Joan Grande

2. Cancer

3. June 26

4. Brown

5. Lavender

6. Dogs

7. "Tiny Barbecue"

8. His dog, Myron

9. Halloween

10. The ponytail extensions hid the damage done from constantly dying her hair red.

Answer Sheet: Personal Facts 3

1. Ariana Grande: Dangerous Woman Diaries

2. She is vegan

3. Edward Butera – Ariana's full surname is Grande-Butera

4. 12

5. Her mother, Joan

6. 16

7. Sirius Black

8. Her left shoulder

9. Science

10. Justin Timberlake

Answer Sheet: Personal Facts 4

1. Penguin

2. She is hypoglycemic

3. Planet Hollywood, New York

4. Valentine's Day, 14th February

5. Jennette McCurdy

6. A serial killer! We think she's joking

7. 1 million Twitter followers

8. Marilyn Monroe and Audrey Hepburn

9. Stuffed animals, hockey pucks and Halloween masks

10. Scooter Braun

Answer Sheet: Collaborations/Duets 1

1. Lady Gaga

2. Break Your Heart Right Back

3. Stuck With U

4. Bang Bang

5. Mika

6. Beauty and the Beast

7. Iggy Azalea

8. Boyfriend

9. Good As Hell

10. Bed

Answer Sheet: Collaborations/Duets 2

1. Victoria Monet

2. Faith

3. Macy Gray

4. Love Me Harder

5. The Way

6. Jessie J

7. Idina Menzel

8. Missy Elliott

9. Cashmere Cat

10. A$AP Ferg

Answer Sheet: Acting

1. 13

2. Cat Valentine

3. Victorious

4. Chanel #2

5. Princess Diaspro

6. Swindle

7. Penny Pingleton

8. 1

9. Zoolander 2

10. Men In Black: International

Answer Sheet: Movie/TV Show Soundtracks

1. Problem

2. Charlie's Angels

3. Miley Cyrus and Lana Del Ray

4. Bang Bang

5. Faith

6. God Is A Woman

7. They Don't Know

8. Honey 3: Dare to Dance

9. Bang Bang

10. Motivation

Answer Sheet: Merchandise

1. Cloud Macchiato

2. Ari by Ariana Grande

3. September 16, 2015

4. Thank U, Next

5. Cloud

6. Thank U, Next

7. Sweet Like Candy

8. $150 million

9. Moonlight

10. Cloud by Ariana Grande

Answer Sheet: Famous Friends 1

1. Elizabeth (Liz) Gillies

2. Katy Perry

3. Pete Davidson

4. Billie Eilish

5. Miley Cyrus

6. Big Sean

7. Elizabeth (Liz) Gillies

8. Justin Bieber

9. Florence Pugh

10. Jim Carrey

Answer Sheet: Famous Friends 2

1. Nicki Minaj

2. Victoria Justice

3. Victoria Monet

4. Side To Side

5. Trash

6. Nicki Minaj

7. Elizabeth (Liz) Gillies

8. Elizabeth (Liz) Gillies

9. WeAreStoopKid

10. Ricky Alvarez

Answer Sheet: Songs 1

1. Thank U, Next

2. No Tears Left To Cry

3. God Is A Woman

4. Pete Davidson

5. Problem

6. Santa Tell Me

7. Put Your Hearts Up

8. My Favorite Part

9. Time

10. The Light Is Coming

Answer Sheet: Songs 2

1. Shangela

2. Bloodline

3. No Tears Left To Cry

4. Thank U, Next

5. Honeymoon Avenue (5 minutes, 39 seconds)

6. Lovin' It (3 minutes)

7. Ghostin (4 minutes, 31 seconds)

8. Makeup (2 minutes, 20 seconds)

9. Break Your Heart Right Back (4 minutes, 13 seconds)

10. Intro (1 minute, 19 seconds)

Answer Sheet: Songs 3

1. Get Well Soon (5 minutes, 22 seconds)

2. Raindrops (An Angel Cried) (38 seconds)

3. Knew Better/Forever Boy (4 minutes, 59 seconds)

4. I Don't Care (2 minutes, 58 seconds)

5. Dangerous Woman

6. These Are A Few Of My Favorite Things, from the Sound of Music soundtrack

7. 32

8. Honeymoon Avenue

9. Break Up With Your Girlfriend, I'm Bored

10. God Is A Woman

Answer Sheet: Albums 1

1. Christmas & Chill

2. Babyface

3. 169,000

4. Yours Truly

5. Dangerous Woman

6. Republic

7. K Bye For Now

8. Daydreamin'

9. 2 weeks

10. 3 years

Answer Sheet: Albums 2

1. Sweetener

2. Sweetener

3. My Everything

4. Sweetener

5. Dangerous Woman

6. Sweetener

7. Sweetener and Thank U, Next

8. 3

9. 12

10. My Everything

Answer Sheet: Music Videos 1

1. Charles Melton

2. Kris Jenner

3. Stuck With U

4. Jonathan Bennett

5. The Young Astronauts

6. Robert Rodriguez

7. 4

8. Side to Side

9. Earth

10. Nicki Minaj

Answer Sheet: Music Videos 2

1. Thank U, Next

2. Toulouse

3. Focus

4. Jennifer Coolidge

5. Stuck With U

6. Rain on Me with Lady Gaga

7. Santa Tell Me

8. Put Your Hearts Up

9. Matt Bennett

10. Side to Side

Answer Sheet: Lyrics 1

1. Problem

2. Side to Side

3. No Tears Left To Cry

4. God Is A Woman

5. Thank U, Next

6. 7 Rings

7. Imagine

8. Break Your Heart Right Back

9. Break Free

10. The Way

Answer Sheet: Lyrics 2

1. Love Me Harder

2. Bed

3. Focus

4. Breakup With Your Girlfriend, I'm Bored

5. Needy

6. Baby I

7. Popular Song

8. Bang Bang

9. Beauty and the Beast

10. Into You

Answer Sheet: Lyrics 3

1. Dangerous Woman

2. R.E.M.

3. Bloodline

4. Put Your Hearts Up

5. Makeup

6. Next

7. Sweetener

8. Rain On Me

9. Santa Tell Me

10. Ghostin

Answer Sheet: Lyrics 4

1. Adore

2. Bad Decision

3. Bad Idea

4. Better Left Unsaid

5. Boyfriend

6. Cadillac Song

7. Daydreamin'

8. In Your Head

9. Fake Smile

10. Get Well Soon

Answer Sheet: Feuds

1. Tekashi 6ix9ine

2. Victoria Justice

3. Kanye West

4. Bette Midler

5. Michael Rappaport

6. Chrissy Teigen

7. Soulja Boy

8. Pete Davidson

9. Little Mix

10. James Charles

Answer Sheet: Awards 1

1. Two

2. Sweetener

3. Problem

4. Top Female Artist

5. The YouTube Music Award

6. Rising Star

7. Thank U, Next

8. Dangerous Woman

9. Best Female Artist

10. Favorite Breakout Artist

Answer Sheet: Awards 2

1. Artist of the Year

2. Cutest Musician

3. Pop Album of the Year

4. Storyteller of the Year

5. Choice SnapChatter

6. Choice Single by a Female Artist

7. Thank U, Next

8. 7 Rings

9. No Tears Left To Cry

10. New Artist of the Year

Answer Sheet: Chart Success

1. 19 minutes

2. Focus

3. 2

4. She was the first artist to have all of her lead singles from her first 3 albums debut in the top 10

5. 3

6. 1

7. Thank U, Next

8. One Last Time

9. 8 weeks

10. Number 2

Answer Sheet: Guest Appearances 1

1. Season 7

2. Family Guy

3. Seahorse

4. Alexa Armstrong

5. Flamingos

6. Jason Robert Brown

7. Seth MacFarlane

8. "That cloud"

9. Kidding

10. The Pickle Fairy

Answer Sheet: Guest Appearances 2

1. Nickelodeon

2. Song Association

3. One Love Manchester

4. Disney Parks Unforgettable Christmas Celebration

5. Jem and the Holograms

6. Global Citizen Festival

7. Three times

8. Twice

9. &Music

10. 12

Answer Sheet: Guest Appearances 3

1. Macy's Front Row Fashion

2. 2014

3. "Awesome"

4. Elsa Hosk

5. Jennifer Lawrence

6. What Will My Scandal Be?

7. This Is Not A Feminist Song

8. Ariana Grande

9. She-ra

10. March Madness

Answer Sheet: Quotes 1

1. Problem

2. Dangerous Woman

3. No Tears Left To Cry

4. Something new.

5. Love

6. Flaws

7. Boring

8. Compassion

9. Quirks

10. Hate

Answer Sheet: Quotes 2

1. The thrill of not knowing what's going to happen

2. Take responsibility and forgive yourself

3. Respect

4. Focus on something beautiful

5. Peace

6. Genius

7. Seriously

8. Like the best version of yourself

9. Care

10. Wear whatever you want

Answer Sheet: Cat Valentine

1. Two – Victorious and Sam & Cat

2. Her nonna

3. Purple

4. Sam Puckett

5. Jade West

6. Robbie Shapiro

7. Goldie Hawn

8. Open doors

9. Toast

10. Three times

Answer Sheet: Diva Behaviour

1. Left

2. Lea Michele

3. Selena Gomez

4. Naya Rivera

5. She didn't show up

6. Giuliana Rancic

7. Alex DeLeon

8. Jennette McCurdy

9. A drawing of Ariana Grande

10. She wanted them to die

Answer Sheet: Miscellaneous 1

1. Keke Palmer

2. Dinosaurs

3. Camilla Cabello

4. Lady Gaga

5. Rihanna

6. Emma Roberts

7. Lucy Hale

8. Bernie Sanders

9. Miley Cyrus

10. Don't Look Back In Anger

Answer Sheet: Miscellaneous 2

1. 55,000

2. The victims and families affected by the bombing at Ariana's Manchester concert on May 22, 2017

3. Somewhere Over The Rainbow

4. 12

5. 13

6. Curly

7. 8

8. 2009

9. 2007

10. Imogen Heap

Answer Sheet: Anagrams

Can you scramble these Ariana song titles?

1. Forecast Rottenly = No Tears Left to Cry

2. Marveled Hero = Love Me Harder

3. Mania Dogs Ow = God is a Woman

4. Babysat Heated Tune = Beauty and the Beast

5. Hosting = Ghostin

6. A Free Kerb = Break Free

7. No Hotdogging = Goodnight N Go

8. Extant Hunk = Thank U, Next

9. Dab Aide = Bad Idea

10. Iron Mane = Rain on Me

If you've enjoyed the book, please leave a review on Amazon: it only takes a minute and it really helps me to continue doing this! Take care - Alex.

Printed in Great Britain
by Amazon